James Hamilton

# This is Not Your Parent's Retirement

## How to Win the Race to Retirement

# This is Not Your Parent's Retirement

James Hamilton

Published by LBD Media Co, 2021.

While every precaution has been taken in the preparation of this book, the publisher assumes no responsibility for errors or omissions, or for damages resulting from the use of the information contained herein.

THIS IS NOT YOUR PARENT'S RETIREMENT

**First edition. March 15, 2021.**

ISBN: 978-1393860471

Written by James Hamilton.

# Disclaimer

━━━

THIS BOOK IS MEANT to offer insights into financial strategies and tax-free options that are available to consumers. It is by no means a substitute for financial advice that one can best receive from a qualified financial advisor.

# From Veteran to Financial Advocate

———

"Knowing is not enough. We must apply.

Willing is not enough. We must do."

*~Bruce Lee*

I GREW UP IN AN ENVIRONMENT where your chances of seeing or experiencing success were slim. There were few role models for good, but many temptations to accept poverty or make bad choices. To many, this story is typical of a kid from the projects, but I have never strived to be typical. From the time I became aware of how different the lives of people outside the projects were, I grew committed to creating a different outcome for my life.

My mother lived a life of constant struggle. She tried hard and worked endlessly, raising three kids with a minimal education and with no noticeable pathway to walk her out of poverty. Viewing her struggles, I thought, "That's just the way life is."

Until one day, I glimpsed a different world than I'd been exposed to before. I saw a life that existed with happiness, a lack of fear, familial and financial stability, and, the real enticement for a young kid, possessions.

I played Little League baseball and became good friends with Kevin, the son of our team's coach. When I went to his house to hang out for the first time, I was immersed in a much different environment from any of the kids from in my neighborhood. It was amazing!

As I drank in this new environment, I learned that my coach was a business guy. From the lifestyle I saw, he was obviously successful. I'd only speculated about Coach and his family being well off up to that point, but when I saw the results his success delivered to his family, I immediately took note of the stark contrast between my world and theirs.

Theirs seemed a lot better.

They had toys, a swimming pool, new cars and a big house (at least compared to the small apartment I lived in). I didn't see obvious stress about the day-to-day aspects of life, like paying bills. That lack of concern contrasted with the worry I often saw in my mother's eyes.

How did they do it?

Before this pivotal experience, I'd never been teased by a flicker of hope that I could, through hard work, live a life that great. The visual of what they had, colliding with the spark of a dream, made an instant impression on me. I couldn't help but think, "If this guy has a business and can live this lifestyle, count me in. That's the direction I want to go."

I saw a formula that showed me how owning a successful business equaled earning enough money for a good lifestyle.

This life-altering moment allowed me to see more than I'd ever seen before, or even thought possible for a 'kid like me'. My horizons instantly expanded, and I sensed the importance of a bigger picture that stemmed from the consequences of all my actions.

After that revelation, what I recognized as possible kept me more focused and grounded, making it easier to avoid the distractions of the environment in which I lived.

Then a second pivotal life moment occurred, that showed me a tangible route to success.

My Uncle Parker, who had been in the military, retired from that career and began to work for the federal government. He drove the car he wanted to drive and had found a way to escape the poverty that so many felt was inevitable. He began to experience more out of life. He did what I wanted to do, which made a large enough impression on me that I wanted to know everything I could about how he'd done it.

Through our talks, my uncle planted a seed in my head that the military was a good option for anyone who wanted to escape the environment in which they lived. My buddy Mike and I agreed with him and we began planning right away, making the commitment that no matter what, when we reached the age of eighteen, we would enlist in the Army, our escape route.

My two pivotal moments began working together and revealed exciting opportunities. I took advantage of every program the Army offered to gain the information and insights necessary to become a business owner.

There are a great many benefits that enlisted people can take advantage of. For me, the different workshops, organizations, and conferences drew me in. This is when I was introduced to MLMs (multi-level marketing) and direct sales. I found a platform in which I could learn and begin my education about being self-employed and connecting with people on a level that created meaning.

I stumbled upon something else highly impactful then, just as it is today. You see, while these forums were beneficial, I used the books, tapes, and other powerful materials that were recommended for self-improvement to really cement in in my mind how to harness my greatest potential. The thought of growing into a better man and by using these resources excited me. I created a better mindset for myself and also saw how much people who did not have a positive mindset struggled.

While mindset is important for everyone, for me mindset became imperative because I had to work past the environment from which I came. I'd seen more struggles than triumphs around me my entire life and those visuals, along with the hard fact that so many people experienced really tough times, had to be shifted to tangible hope for something more. Yes, there were lessons and motivations in those challenges, yet I never realized how much those same challenges had impacted my mental process until it was revealed to me during this learning opportunity.

What we believe in our mind is what is possible. This is why we have to believe in good outcomes and learn how to create our actions based on those desired good outcomes.

My work ethic and commitment to what I wanted to do have always been strong for me. Those things helped me keep my conviction about what I wanted to achieve, while also guiding me to keep working hard to achieve those goals. The military gave me a perfect backdrop to further strengthen these intuitive skills.

Around the time of my basic training, the Gulf War and Operation Desert Storm began, quickly altering the landscape of my military career. Even during this time, I continued to learn. Through the intensity of our missions, the skills to plan and implement strategies for specific outcomes were essential.

Being a 'boots on the ground' guy meant that I had to take the urban jungle I grew up in and transfer those survival skills to the desert combat zone.

During my time in the military I participated in combat missions and also worked in peace-keeping zones. Each experience heightened my awareness about every detail of the world around me and also gave me a strong appreciation for strategic planning.

Although I was unaware of it at the time, gaining these experiences served as a catalyst for my journey into the financial services industry. A lack of planning can be devastating and detrimental to your life in many different environments.

After proudly serving my country for eight years, I decided to not re-enlist. I didn't know what my return to civilian life would include, but I did know that one of the biggest challenges many veterans faced was finding a position where they could make as much money as they did while they were enlisted. In order to make the income I wanted, I knew I would have to be in a position where I would be paid based on my effort.

The job I decided to take was in sales, a position that up-sold services. It provided me with a decent income, but I lacked the financial acumen necessary to make smartest choices with my money. These absent skills included: budgeting, saving, spending habit considerations, etc. I sensed this, and it brought to light two important points for me to focus on.

First, I should work on changing my mindset about money and how to make my paycheck work most effectively for me.

Second, the person who benefited the most from my sales efforts was the owner of the company, not me. The guy winning is the guy at the top.

All of this reiterated that I needed to really commit to becoming a true entrepreneur. I truly wanted to be the guy at the top. I began pursuing an opportunity, based on a simple, three-part plan.

1.  Come up with an idea.
2.  Work hard, taking the appropriate risks necessary to grow the business.
3.  Sell the business at the 'right time' and retire, living out my remaining years comfortably.

I did those things and my plan worked, but what drew me in most were the ways in which money worked behind success. From there, a natural transition into the financial services industry followed. I felt convicted that other people needed to know this stuff, too, especially the underserved black business-owning community.

I paid attention to how finances impacted everything. They could build you up quickly and tear you down even faster. But not if you were prepared.

# Numbers Don't Lie

―――

"Only buy something that you'd be perfectly happy

to hold if the market shut down for 10 years."

*~Warren Buffet*

IMAGINE YOU STARTED with an investment of $100,000 in 1987. That value would have dropped to $73,000 after the crash of 1987. If you remained invested after that, the $73,000 would have grown to $421,000 by January 2000. These raw numbers reveal why the 1990s were one of the hottest decades in the history of the stock market.

Again, if you had remained fully invested, your $421,000 would have decreased to $126,363 by July 2002, during the 'Dot Com Crash'. Staying fully invested, that $126,363 would have grown to $237,562 by October 2007. After the 'Credit Crash' of 2007 and 2008, that $237,562 would have decreased to $104,527. Staying fully invested after TARP and all other government stimulus used during the last decade, your $104,527 would have rebuilt itself to $318,808 today.

If we were to have another crash and the market lost even 30%, that number would decline to $212,538. Or if the decline was 50%, you'd be looking at $159,404. Your original $100,000 would only have doubled over the last thirty years for an average return of around 2.5% annually.

Before taxes and fees.

In another scenario, imagine the market lost 50% in the next downturn. In this case, you'd only have 60% of a double in 30 years, making for an annual average return for 1.5%.

These numbers could be worse. Why? Because many people lost extensively before exiting the market. Then, being fearful, they did not return to the market to enjoy the following growth until very late in the cycle. I believe many Americans have still not made back what they lost between 2000-2002 and the 2007 and 2008 downturns.

Now, just for fun, let's examine what happened to the same $100,000 investment in 1987 if you missed the three crashes.

1. From November of 1987 to January of 2000 your $100,000 grows to $416,470.
2. From July of 2002 to September 0f 2007 your $416,470 grows to $782,963.
3. From March of 2009 to the present your $782,963 grows to $2.12 million dollars.

Amazing! Of course, this is only in theory. No one will ever get this exactly right. However, what this example shows us the methodology behind 'buying low and selling high'.

Contemplate these questions:

- Would this strategy have worked far better than staying fully invested?
- Isn't this timing the market? I would argue it is not.

We are not adjusting for every little market turn. These are essentially five course adjustments in thirty years with a sixth about to happen.

What if there was a way you could develop a strategy to help you lose little or nothing and have access to your money, liquidity, and take advantage of downturns after they happen? Couldn't a strategy like that be performed more confidently?

Think about this: that initial $100,000 invested in 1987 is currently valued at $318,808. Even without a crash that money tripled over a thirty-year period. Using the rule of 115, that is, how many years it takes for money to triple the average annual return would be less than 4%.

There are many fixed interest investments I could have offered my prospects along that thirty-year journey that would have yielded more than 4% without any of the risk. Indexing strategies keep your money safe during downturns yet allow for withdrawals to take advantage of positive market moves. This type of strategy is highly suitable for the times in which we find ourselves.

Let's begin with global debt. In 2007, the world debt total was $142 trillion dollars. By 2014, that debt had risen to $199 trillion, an increase of $57 trillion (40%) in just seven years.

Forward three years. The world debt increases to $300 trillion, a 50% increase. That increase in debt sustains our stock, bond, and commodities markets. That debt must be serviced. You begin to see bankruptcies everywhere, not just companies, countries are going bankrupt, too, and that will continue. The World Economic Forum just announced that they believe there will be a $400 trillion savings shortfall by 2050.

This information tells us that we can both learn from the past and do better in the future.

America's Social Security Board of Trustees says the trust-fund backing Social Security will be exhausted by 2035; this after an eight-year bull market. If we have the downturn that is expected, that year could be moved up to as soon as 2025. Proposed House legislation, (the Social Security 2100 Act) would increase the FICA tax from 6.2% to 7.4% and would completely phase out the $127,200 ceiling on earnings that are subject to payroll tax. That is a tax increase of 19% on every working man, woman, and child in the United States.

Government requires increasingly more revenues to fund the future. Even President Trump's current budget is an increase. The current budget is $4.062 trillion. The president's budget is $4.094 trillion. The annual deficit will approach one trillion and rise exponentially in the years ahead.

This will make it harder to save for the future. More difficult to pass on wealth generationally. The government will require more and more tax revenue. You can find the foundational information for this discussion at www.usdebtclock.org[1]. The clock shows there are around 50 million people currently on Social Security.

All of these overwhelming, hard to process numbers reveal how we struggle to come up with the money to provide Social Security and Medicare to these 50 million people.

About thirteen years from now, in the year 2030, we will have between 80 and 90 million people receiving Social Security and Medicare with 70% of the Baby Boomers turning 65 between 2022 and 2029. That's a little more than a decade. Where will the government find the revenue to meet these financial requirements for Social Security and Medicare? And, more realistically, should we rely on the government to provide these funds, knowing that something will have to give?

Next consider that there are bubbles in our economy that will burst at some point, even if we don't know precisely when.

1.  Housing Bubble: The United State, Canada, and China are all facing serious housing bubbles. China's crisis widely considered to be the biggest housing bubble in the history of the world. Housing prices in Canada, especially in Toronto and Vancouver, are off the charts. There is also an enormous amount of speculation in the U.S. housing market. Many analysts

---

1. http://www.updebtclock.org/

predict crashes.

2. Debt Bubble: the whole world is in debt up to their eyeballs. This will not diminish but increase dramatically. Again, China appears to be the biggest debt bubble in the history of the world. Nobody is sure what will happen when this debt bubble bursts, but all agree it will not be good.

3. Corporate Debt Bubble: in the next three years, a lot of debt will require refinancing. Analysts expect quite a bit to default with projected losses of $1.5 to $2 trillion in in the next three years. What impact will this have?

4. Commercial Real Estate Bubble: almost all commercial real estate needs to be refinanced in the next 4 years. How many of these properties won't appraise out because they don't have tenants? How many vacant units so we see all over the country? Consider the effect on the world economy.

5. Silicon Valley Bubble: everything in Silicon Valley is overpriced and when the crash comes, an area like this will be devastated. Bubbles usually burst in a bigger fashion than they did previously. They essentially revert to their mean prices.

6. Tech Bubble: many analysts fear we will see another bubble like the one that burst between 2000 and 2002. Many stocks prices are not supported by real earnings. When people start to realize this, they head for the door very quickly.

    a. Bursting bubbles send the markets into chaos, as history has proven. But there is even more to take into consideration.

7. Further complicating things is the fact that stocks are being purchased using more margin than ever in history. Now over one half trillion of margin is being used. Can you spell disaster?

8. The United States has very serious issues. Student loan debt, now at $1.4 trillion and rising, while more and more of this debt falls into default. Over one million people have not paid anything on their student loans in over a year.

9. Auto industry debt is now at $1.1 trillion and rising. Much of this is subprime debt that will never be paid back. Imagine having to bail out General Motors and Chrysler again, and this time we will have to add Ford to the list.

10. Credit card debt is now over $1 trillion dollars. We are essentially back to where we were before 2007 and 2008.

11. Many people now have enormous medical debt because of the much higher deductibles and lower co-pays on health insurance. This amount will increase exponentially as we continue to diminish the quality of our health insurance.

12. Finally, pensions in our country are a mess. Chicago's workers' pension only has enough money to last seven more years. Most pensions at the state, county, city and municipality level are dramatically underfunded and getting worse by the minute. Americans will panic when they find out what terrible financial shape their pensions are in. This information could be the surprise

contributing factor to the next downturn.

Put this is the 'did you know' category:

- 50% of Americans arrive at death or retirement with nothing saved?
- 70% of Americans arrive at death or retirement with less than $28,000?
- After an eight-year bull market, 90% of Americans still have less than $115,000 saved. And, according to Fidelity Investments, the largest 401K provider by triple, they just reported that the average 401(k) balance at their firm is $92,500. Think about this: if you live to age 95 and only have $92,500 in a 401(k), what kind of retirement do you have?
- If the government desperately needs more revenue in the future, what will the 90% of Americans who have no money do? If you're in the 10% who have money, are you okay with the government coming and taking your money to take care of people who were not willing to save and invest the way you did?

It is good to remember that the richest generation by age group is grandmas and grandpas. They lived through the Great Depression and became wealthy because they were great savers, not great investors. They also learned to live within their means. This will happen again after the next downturn. Is it time for the history lesson to be repeated?

Even on the heels of all this news, please, don't panic! I want to very clearly say that none of this is bad news. It's not good news, either. It's just news, information. There is no 'end of world' scenario.

If you plan and prepare using this information, it can provide opportunity of a lifetime. If you don't plan and prepare, your finances may be devastated. The choice is yours.

# Understanding Your Parent's Retirement

---

"Often when you think you're at the end of something,

you're at the beginning of something else."

*~Fred Rogers*

THE CONCEPT OF WORKING hard, saving, and investing wisely so you can relax and enjoy retirement is more complex than when most of our parents eased into their pre-retirement years.

Most of our parents went to high school, trained for a skill, worked at their job, took advantage of a pretty decent market, and then retired happy. Their entire retirement strategy was based on a three-system cash flow. Think of it like a stool: a three-legged stool is sturdy. This is the basic retirement planning model that was taught. It included:

1. Personal savings that are available for use when necessary.
2. A pension benefit that was reflective of a certain portion of an employee's salary that they earned upon their retirement.
3. Social Security Income (SSI) is what the government pays upon retirement, based on you paid based on your pre-retirement earnings.

This sturdy stool worked ideally for many people, making retirement a sure deal. It was a no brainer. Everything worked out as planned. The market wasn't prone to large fluctuations and the guaranteed income offered stability and assurance to people retiring. Since this system worked, it really never needed to be questioned.

It was ideal. So, what's the problem now? Why did everything change?

The problems that lead to the unraveling of our parents' pathways to retirement began in corporate America. The businesses who offered pensions began experiencing a shift in how long people lived. With this longevity came a harsh realization that they could no longer afford pension plans for their retired workers. The plans caused them to go broke and then, out of business.

While this is logical in hindsight, the big challenge that stemmed from this demographic shift was that there was never a comparable change to retrain the population into a new, sustainable way to properly retire. Our parents taught us the only thing they knew, but their plan no longer applied to us. We only received a two-legged stool. Take a moment to visualize how well that would work. If it seems impossible to you, you're right.

# The Reality of 401(k) and Social Security Income

"Retirement is like a long vacation in Las Vegas.

The goal is to enjoy it to the fullest,

but not so fully than you run out of money."

*~Jonathan Clements*

MOST PEOPLE ALIGN A 401(k) with their retirement planning, which can be a highly effective tool that works very well for them. However, the money is still invested in the market, which means puts their funds at risk.

The condition of many peoples' 401(k)s is likely to be more favorable if they are working with an advisor who is proactive in taking on the challenges that come with the market. Without a doubt, the market is highly effective for long-term growth. However, the market and a 401(k) should never be a singular strategy for retirement.

401(k)s present a big challenge on the fee side, moreso than the growth side. The fees will eat you alive and you may not even realize what's happening until it's too late. If you have a fee, even one that seems low, (such as 2%) that amount isn't a big deal when you open the account. But how about after you begin accumulating?

Remember, 401(k) accounts are tax deferred accounts. This means that after you pay all your taxes, fees, and other expenses, your $400,000 account could only net you $200,000.

This is a lot of money for most of us, and what really startles folks about the situation is that many do not know this could happen and by the time they find out, it's both shocking and too late. I spend a lot of time discussing this situation during the seminars I present. I call it the "Tax Bomb Shell" and if you don't detonate the bomb on your own, it's going to blow up in your face at some point.

Now you know the risks of your 401(k) a bit better. Do you think you've still got retirement covered because you'll receive Social Security Income?

While Social Security Income will likely never go away, most analysts project that the majority of retirees will allocate their entire SSI to the cost of their healthcare.

Unless our healthcare system gets fixed quickly, which is fairly unlikely, this expense is something you need to plan for. Ideally, in order to maximize your SSI, you want to wait to start making withdrawals as late as possible. Currently, 71½ years of age is the longest you can wait. By waiting this long, you can receive as high of a percentage as available and cross your fingers the funds last as long as you do.

What I find encouraging is that where there is 401(k) and Social Security Income uncertainty, there is also a stable option that is beneficial: tax-free retirement planning. This strategy goes against what most of us have been taught and many do not even realize this is another option. I'm here to tell you it's a great option that can change your retirement picture for the better, offering you stability through a tactical approach.

# Tax Free Retirement Planning: The Basics

———

"Instead of worrying about what you cannot control,

shift your energy to what you can create."

*~Roy T. Bennett*

MOST OF YOU ARE THINKING, "Tax-free sounds impossible." Most of us have been taught that taxes are unavoidable, an inevitable part of investing and retiring.

Taxes are scary mostly because there are no guarantees they will even remain at the same rate you prepare for. Tax rates from when you're twenty will not be the same as when you are sixty-five, and while we like to think taxes may go down, it contradicts with our desires to have our income go up because more income means higher taxes.

So, what's the answer? What you really need is tax-free growth.

Tax-free growth takes place when you allow your money to grow in the market, while it is not actually in the market.

This method, which allows people to benefit from tax-free growth, lies in something that has existed for extended periods of time: approaching finances like insurance companies approach their investments. With this approach you are taking after-tax dollars and allowing them to grow tax-free income in an efficient manner. And you can make withdrawals tax-free. How is this possible?

As it turns out, the significant market events aren't quite as unpredictable as most people have been led to believe.

There is an entire area of finance that revolves around tax-free retirement and it's not fully tapped into. Tax-free retirement products offer a better option by allowing someone to grow money without risking substantial losses. It is a great disservice for an advisor to allow any individual to think that having a 401(k) and pension plan means they "have retirement covered".

Because of what I'd gone through with my own business, I have a connectivity to other business owners and have found it to be a much-underserved market, particularly in the African American community, where incredible entrepreneurs are involved in amazing endeavors. By helping these business owners, I am also helping their employees and their families. Everyone benefits, or at least has access to knowledge about the pertinent information that may give them a chance to be less impacted by those "unanticipated market shifts" that have become commonplace in U.S. markets.

The decisions that must be made need to be based on risk. The three areas that factor into total risk: tax risk, market risk, and structure risk.

# Tax Risk

WITHOUT A DOUBT, THE biggest risk all of us face involves our tax risk. Every economic bracket and career is subject to tax risk, and it's one of those risks over which we feel we have little control. For some things, this may be true, but when it comes to retirement, you have more control than you think.

For Generation X (those born from 1961-1981), this is particularly important to understand. These people are in prime retirement planning years and financial decisions made today matter.

A majority of people save in vehicles that defer taxes, but don't really understand what that means for their retirement income.

Ask yourself this question: are my taxes going to be higher, the same, or lower in the future? And, how do you guarantee your answer?

The whole concept of building a 401(k) or any qualified plan is based on lower taxes in the future. This provides a challenge because if you look at our country today, as well as our current tax code, you will find something shocking. We are in one of the lowest tax brackets since 1913. This is due to the resistance to raising taxes. No politician wants to be the one who raised taxes. Mentioning it has cost people elections.

Strangely enough, despite the resistance to raise taxes, most people believe taxes are going to increase over time, not decrease, and they feel the main problem is Uncle Sam's spending habits. It's hard to argue this point, but it's based on a feeling.

With our big deficit, what does Uncle Sam have to bank on to keep things going? Your retirement that hasn't been taxed yet, that's what.

The government knows who has qualified plans that are tax-deferred and what is eventually due to them down to the penny. They are vested in paying close attention to these future funds because the state of financial affairs for our government is troublesome.

To give you some perspective, a few years ago, analysts declared a victory when the federal deficit was the first increase less than one trillion dollars in five years. Analysts saw that as a good sign. For your average business owner or individual tax payer, it's hard to see any reason to celebrate such a thing. One trillion dollars is an exorbitant amount of money that barely registers on most peoples' perspective scale.

Now, put yourself into the scenario of living in Greece. One of the largest challenges their economy faced before its collapse was increasing taxes three times within ten years. People couldn't afford the increase, which shifted any type of stability almost any average income earner nearing retirement previously relied on.

Imagine you have half a million dollars in your qualified plan and you choose the age sixty-five to retire. Generally, your house will be paid off and your kids grown and gone. The retirement model assumes these two things are in place even though this is hardly the case all of the time, for various reasons.

However, if you are fortunate and have your home paid off and your kids have flown the coop, you discover you are losing one of the biggest tax deductions in America. When your kids leave home and become independent of you, another significant tax deduction is gone. In fact, those things may put you into a higher tax bracket.

Now we have an increasingly serious problem with that half million dollars in your qualified retirement plan. You have paid no taxes, you have fewer deductions, and you're moved up an income bracket. Three things suddenly become a major concern:

1.  Making too much money (as illogical as this seems).
2.  Your pension, because what you net can be extensively different than your pre-tax balance.
3.  New taxes you may not have considered.

When do you pay taxes? Do you pay on the seed or the harvest? You're an apple farmer and you plant a single seed and harvest ten apples. The auditor shows up and says that you have one opportunity to determine how to pay your taxes. What do you do? Do you pay taxes on the seed upfront, or pay taxes on the harvest at a later date?

If you pay taxes on the seed, you will only pay on what you plant. This means that one apple seed will produce ten apples for you, but you're only paying on that one seed. If the seed costs you $1.00 you will owe 30¢ if you are in the 30% tax bracket. You can sell each apple for a dollar, knowing your taxes were paid when you paid for the seed.

With the 'pay later' option, you'll pay taxes on your harvest. Using the same scenario, you have a seed that costs you $1.00, and you decide to save now and pay later. You plant the seed and defer the 30% in taxes for the future. Harvest time comes, and you have ten amazing apples, paying 30% tax on each one, which comes to $3.00 per apple, leaving a profit of $7.00, compared to 30% off a single dollar for the seed.

Who benefits from waiting to pay later? The government. They want you to pay on the harvest, but you don't have to. Furthermore, ponder this: when is the government going to need more money, today or tomorrow?

Baby boomers are still working at a 5:1 work ratio today. They are the largest population in our history and when they begin to retire, it's estimated that there will be a 2:1 work ratio. This puts a great deal of stress on the Social Security system.

The government is going to need more money to sustain its Social Security obligations as this generation retires. This, in turn, increases the probability of raising taxes.

The buzz word in media is that only the rich will be taxed, not the middle class or poor. However, most money is hosted by the middle class. They have 401(k) accounts, not rich people. The wealthy use an informed tax system, knowing the best way to maximize their dollars by paying taxes on their investments at the best time.

It may be natural to feel frustrated by those who know how to maximize their income and reduce or eliminate taxes, but such maneuvers are completely legal and within their rights. Sadly, I've seen individuals who chose to defer $75K and wait to pay it later be shocked to realize that they were suddenly paying $475K in taxes right at the wrong time, as they prepare to retire.

What makes the most sense to you? Tax-free strategies don't have to be a rich man's game. Those same strategies can be used to keep you richer than you might be otherwise.

## Market Risk

MARKET RISK CAN PRESENT a few challenges. Placing your money into the market is inherently risky. It's a common practice and one of those things most people have heard they need to do to earn money. Wall Street is built on encouraging this activity. Yes, it can build wealth, but what about the instability factors involved in the market?

You must assess market stability against where you are in your retirement planning.

Retirement planning has three phases. Each phase has a significant function in your retirement strategies and the decisions made within that period of time.

*Phase One: Accumulation*

This is where you are saving and investing, possibly taking some higher risks to build your portfolio more quickly. If there is a market downturn and you lose, you have a chance to rebound and rebuild before facing the potentially serious risk you won't have enough money to retire with the same lifestyle you currently enjoy.

*Phase Two: Preservation*

These are the years we refer to as the "red zone". You are ten years away from retiring, and it's time to move your investments from high or mid risk to low risk. This is a concept that most informed investors embrace. Your goal is to not suffer any significant losses you cannot afford or jeopardize the lifestyle you seek during retirement.

*Phase Three: Distribution*

This phase happens when you retire and begin drawing on your income. You want your payments to replace your salary in a combination of your savings, Social Security Income, and distribution from your retirement-specific account(s).

Equate retirement planning to owning a yacht. You go through your days, months, and years putting gasoline into that yacht, fueling it up much like your investments fuel your retirement account. The yacht is in motion and, if it gets caught in a storm, it keeps going, handing the weather (the market).

As time goes on, you move into the red zone, and the last thing you want in that final decade of your pre-retirement game is to have your yacht damaged by a Hurricane Katrina. If your yacht is worth $100K and you sustain $40K worth of damage, what are your chances of getting that money back before your distribution phase begins? Pretty slim.

On average, recovering from market loss takes about ten years, and you don't have that much time any longer.

So, what do you do? Do you invest to fix your yacht (a.k.a the market loss)? If you do, are you looking at positioning your retirement with a lesser lifestyle than you initially desired? Are you willing to, and can you work past your initial retirement date to help at least break even from the loss?

These are choices you need to make if this happens and knowing the best way to do this with the least amount of tax repercussions is important. But also remember that it could have been avoided with the right strategy on the front end.

Market risk depends on markets correcting, but this is unpredictable. We just know correction eventually happens. What happens if you retired September 2008, and the market corrects 37% in a short window of time? What are the chances of you being able to take distributions during retirement that align with your current lifestyle? The odds are not in your favor, according to most analysts.

The 2008 market crash wiped out many retirement accounts. Rebounding markets that occur near our retirement date affect us. So, market risk is a greater threat when you are nearing distribution than any other time. These events can literally wipe out your retirement income if you do not have it placed in the proper risk category.

Anyone who works in the financial field knows 2000-2009 is an example of what happens when the market takes unexpected twists and turns. People who wanted to retire during this time understand the harsh impact reflected on traditional retirement planning methods. Today, we are not even ten years away from the worst decade in stock market history. Much heartache could have been avoided if people used the strategies that come from tax-free retirement planning.

# Structure Risk

HOW YOU ARE SAVING? Most individuals only understand one way to save, and this ties back into this "it's not your parent's retirement" example. You simply can't end up with a three-legged retirement stool in your retirement structure by default any longer. You need to take specific steps to gain this kind of stability.

The structure of risk today is that most of us only have one leg, not two or three.

A few careers still give someone access to a traditional retirement plan, such as military and government employees. But this is a unique individual, hardly a representation of a majority of future retirees.

The structure risk we face today is that most people are singular in their structure. They have a contribution plan with their 401(k) or other qualified account. They put their money in, maybe it's matched by their employer, and then they leave it there, assuming that it's the best deal because growth is the quickest. Of course, there's value to these plans but you need to be more diverse. The time has come to be more mindful of what you are doing right now and what those actions mean for tomorrow.

You should strive instead to create a balanced cash flow system for retirement.

The insights and strategies to create balance come from a meaningful interaction and evaluation of your current portfolio with a financial advisor who can focus on ways to preserve what you're building and offer ways to minimize risk. It's not that you'll never lose anything, but you increase the odds you won't go backward.

When you eventually reach retirement, the most valuable thing you have is not the size of the assets, but the guarantee of the distribution.

I believe you should consider leaving Social Security Income as a mechanism to pay for healthcare. This means your personal savings and retirement plans should address all other cash flow needed to retire at a certain level.

Whatever you choose to do, you'd be best served to realize that if you try to accumulate during your distribution phase, you're absolutely going about the process in the wrong way. We are at a time in our world when we need to take control of our retirement and how events will unfold for us in the years we plan to draw from money from those accounts.

# Tactical, Indexing, and Tax-free Strategies

———

"You don't pay taxes. They take taxes."

*~Chris Rock*

MOST PEOPLE DON'T QUESTION if they should have insurance because they see how the coverage protects them. They purchase insurance for their car, their health, their home, their life, and many other things. However, they hardly ever think of insurance in regard to their largest asset, their retirement. Tactical investing creates an insurance component to this valuable asset.

When you invest monies on indexing strategies, the money is not 'in the market', it's 'against the market'. This means that a cap is set for the maximum and minimum index. You can only anticipate the cap through the use of software. Maybe it's 12% high and 0% low, which means that if the market goes negative you're capped at no growth. You never lose money. Zero's your hero!

These strategies are not best used as an 'all in' option, but you should smartly allocate a portion of your retirement assets.

By considering a portion of your investable monies for insurance investing and other types of alternative markets, you eliminate a major decision who invests in the standard markets: when do you buy, sell, or stay put?

It's easy to feel that pit in your stomach when you see the market going up and down and you know those changes are linked to what your future looks like. You can end up driving yourself crazy and as a result, you may make rash decisions in the moment that are not good for you long-term. With insurance investing, you can feel confident you won't lose anything with that money, protecting your retirement wellbeing. The tactical strategy is what will lessen the risk of loss.

## Tactical Strategies

A TACTICAL STRATEGY involves you giving your money manager the ability to make predictions that give them insight about when to get out, often months before a market crashes. This is done using software and the money manager's sole job is to evaluate what is happening within your parameters and make any required adjustments. These programs constantly monitor the algorithm you set up and make determinations based on performance history in the market. This insight allows your invested funds to be best protected.

Here are two things to note about this process. First, your financial advisor doesn't do the day-to-day managing of money. We mostly park the funds with money managers, as they invest and monitor market activities. We research various broker relationships to ensure we are creating the best potential connections for our clients.

Second, as the client, you have access to this information and can see what is happening all of the time. Through this approach, the aspirations that people have with their money can play out in a better way, including important factors that many people used to take for granted. Two great examples are:

1. Paying for your child's college education. Parents used to consider it an honor and a joy to help pay for their children's education. It was the essence of the American dream. Today, college tuition increased 30+% in five years and continues to rise an average of 6% per year. For most parents to help with college today they are required to withdraw from their retirement plans, a scary proposition, if even feasible.

2. Retiring with the same type of lifestyle you currently have. Far too often retirement means downgrading homes, plans for fun, and even the healthcare decisions a person makes. Through better strategies based on today's world realities, this can be circumvented. It all starts with a plan and a partnership with a money manager.

The sooner you become aware of how tactical strategies can help you create a portfolio that will be prepared for you when you enter into your retirement years, the better you can position yourself to live the life you've dreamt of after years of hard work and create the legacy and gifts for your family that may be important to you.

# Indexing Strategies

AN INDEXING STRATEGY is a bit more unique because it allows individuals to get the upside of the market without the downside of the risk. Such strategies include:

- How interest is credited to your policy.
- In a rising market, it will capture a portion of the growth of the index, up to the cap.
- In a falling market, it will not drop past zero growth.

How does this work? By focusing on a couple basic principles:

- Grow with indexing strategies while not being in the market.
- Gains may be exciting (22%, for example) but the worst you can do is 0%. Your risk is negated.

One of the most appealing features of indexing strategies is that it's a great place to park a portion of your assets so you can count on them whenever you need the asset, as there is no negative growth. Another, more practical and necessary feature of indexing strategies is how they help prevent losses when you're in the "red zone" (the preservation phase of your retirement).

With indexing, you'll see the term Indexed Universal Life (IUL), which is the basis for indexing strategies. The tax advantages which IUL's are best noted for include:

- Addressing tax risk by allowing tax-free loans available in retirement.
- Interest earnings are not taxed.
- No penalty for withdrawals before the age 59½.
- No requirement to draw money after 70½.

Because of these benefits, dual protection is offered. IUL's help manage risk three ways. First, by offering death benefits to protect heirs and accumulating value. Second, by having the potential for growth while protecting against the risk of loss, and finally, by giving someone access to tax-free loans.

Today is the day to make these important considerations because each day may end up costing money. Waiting a single year to begin could mean 11% less accumulation. Wait five years and you could be facing a number as high as 40% (percentages are for example only).

## Tax-free Concepts

TAX-FREE CONCEPTS HAVE been around for a long time but have recently been introduced as an investment strategy. They use the same entity, an indexing strategy, but allow you to grow your money inside of an interest contract, so when you grow that money, you're guaranteed tax-free income in the future.

With this strategy, you are allowed to create your own pension plan, the proverbial third leg of the stool. This strategy is on the rise with Generation X, in particular, as they are the first wave of individuals to discover that jobs with pensions are difficult to find.

Using this concept, a personal pension plan is created through someone's own savings strategies, placing the money in a contract typically kept for ten to fifteen years.

Imagine this scenario: you want to accumulate and save money in a safer manner with no downside risk and you want any gains you earn to be tax-free in the future. It's the seed and the harvest principle. If you take what's remaining after you pay and put it into this strategy, you can grow your asset and receive tax-free income. This type of investment is sanctioned by IRS Code 7702, an internal revenue code that allows for this structure exist. This is not a 401(k) or qualified plan, because as the assets accumulate, you still have access to the funds. Additionally, this is the type of account that can provide you with living benefits, should the need arise.

If this type of investment strategy is appealing to you and you want to learn more about it, you'll want to ensure that you go to an advisor who thoroughly understands this concept and its caveats. If not structured properly, this strategy can create a real problem for you. If any advisor you approach is highly versed in this type of transaction, they will easily be able to offer specific insights on these following points:

- They should be able to provide a worst-case scenario

for your specific example. This scenario will include the downside of the concept. The reason this is important is because it is far more likely you'll find an advisor who only shows you the upside. If they do not have the proper software system to show the downside, they are selling you a perfect world projection. We'd all love a 'perfect' investment, but time has shown us to expect ups and downs.

- Request multiple examples of different indexing strategies. More often than not, only a single strategy will be illustrated, but to find out what your best options might be, your advisor should be able to demonstrate multiple examples. Your situation, needs, and goals are unique to you.
- Find out specific information on living benefits. This is so important because you cannot do this in any other qualified plan without paying penalties. That's why it's such a powerful concept.

Despite what people may believe, there are tax-free options that can help maximize your money and minimize your tax liability. They are secure, legal options that may not have all the excitement that comes with playing the market, but they will help take you to your retirement with some assurances that you've got things covered.

If you're still challenged by the thoughts of these different types of strategies, please know this: today, we live in a different America and a new set of challenges exists for Baby Boomers, as well as Generations X and Y, and eventually the Millennials, too. We all get older; the key is to get wiser along the way.

# Case Scenarios for Tax-free Investing

---

"We must care for each other more, and tax each other less."

*~Bill Archer*

WITH THE NEW RULES of savings, you identify your risks and create a strategy to address them. Then you take action, because it's never too early or late to take control of your retirement picture.

And every retirement picture is different, regardless of how much you may appear to have in common with someone else. This is why it's so important to make decisions based on your personal financial picture.

Therefore, the following scenarios are meant to give you an overview of how different retirement scenarios can play out and help you better understand what your decisions today mean to your future retirement income.

## Case Scenario #1: Tom

TOM HAS ALWAYS BEEN a traditional guy, committed to working hard and providing for his family, eager to enter into retirement and improve his golf game, enjoy the grandkids, and finally take that vacation to Italy that he's been promising his wife since their twenty-fifth wedding anniversary.

An overview of Tom: he's a 74-year-old retired executive who has a pension, Social Security, and 401(k) with match.

When we look at Tom, we see his planning thus far is what will carry him through his retirement.

*Assessing risk*: Tom has all three legs of his stool in place—Social Security, personal savings, and employer pension.

Most people are appreciative of how Tom's financial planning looks on the surface. He's done things right—disciplined and committed, taking advantage of the most widely known strategies that have been in place for decades.

*Social Security Income*: Tom is able to collect his Social Security Income, knowing what it will be for the remainder of his retirement.

Because of Tom's age and his lifelong buy-in to Social Security, he is able to have access to this income to contribute not just toward healthcare, but to his lifestyle, as well.

*Tax risk*: Tom is using his funds and they are slowly depleting, leaving him unsure if they are going to last for the duration of his life. If he is blessed with longevity, this could be problematic when he reaches his mid-eighties.

Remember that saving money as tax deferred while planning for retirement means you will pay an unknown portion of taxes when you retire.

This is what Tom's numbers look like for his retirement in the scenario where he deferred taxes (assuming a 33% tax bracket). Remember, this is Tom's example and no basis for you to believe yours would be the same should be implied.

Tom's Asset Savings Timeline

- Contribute $7,500 annually for 30 years
- Tax deferral: $2,500 in taxes annually
- After 30 years: $75,000 in deferred taxes to pay

Tom's Spending Assets Timeline

- Withdraw $75,000 annually for 15 years
- Tax liability: $25,000 per year
- After 15 years: $375,000 in taxes paid

All the paperwork indicated Tom appeared to be set for a great retirement. Until he actually retired and realized his tax liability.

If Tom would have considered other options, such as choosing to pay taxes up-front instead of at retirement, he might have been able to access more of the fruits of his labor.

## Case Scenario #2: Ellen

ELLEN IS A DETERMINED single mother whose husband passed away when her children were just three and one. He didn't leave her financially set, so she had to come up with a plan. Ellen went back to school and graduated in Marketing

& Management at the age of thirty and began investing in the typical retirement options two years later. During this time, she recognized a need to protect her children, should something happen to her.

An overview of Ellen: she is a 52-year-old Marketing Director with a 401(k) (no employer match) and an IRA rollover.

Ellen has some options in place, but she is starting a bit later than some people and has less time to begin building that coveted nest egg.

*Assessing risk*: Ellen's stool is wobbly. She does not have Social Security income yet and no employer matched pension; however, she has personal savings. With no company sponsored plan for Ellen, she has to match 50% funds, compared to either 8% contribution for a private pension or 15% contribution for a 401(k) with a 6% match.

While Ellen was diverted from retirement saving when she was a young mother, she realizes today that retirement is just around the corner and she's within a few years of entering into the "red zone". Being strategic is the best option she has.

*Social Security Income*: since Ellen has many more years of work before she can claim Social Security Income, she is facing an unknown variable. Over time, the number of people in the work force, compared to those who collected the income has reduced from an average of a 5:1 ratio to 2:1.

There is a lot of hype about Social Security Income and what it may either be or not be for those of us who are not yet retired. We want to count on it, have to realize that it's only one leg on the retirement school.

*Market risk*: for Ellen, her risk is ongoing since she is in the accumulation phase for her retirement. She has been advised of the following options:

- 401(k) or Roth 401(k)
- IRA (Individual Retirement Account) or Roth IRA
- Managed account

These are big decisions! Ellen has learned that the market has been the best it has been since 2000 at this time and that the US Treasury Rate has been on a steady decline since 1985.

Sometimes numbers are deceiving when you look at a growth statistic. With all the variables that come into play, Ellen needs to speak with a financial advisor for independent advice on what her best strategies are, given her personal story and timeline.

To defer now or pay now, that is the question. Ellen's potential choices are:

- Pay $375,000.00 at retirement.
- Pay now and enjoy tax-free later on.

Weighing out what's convenient, most common, or even suggested in one moment against what really best provides for you during your retirement years is a tough question. Ellen has agreed to consider both options, as she has two kids and hopes of being able to do great things for her grandchildren someday.

Life is going to have risks, but you can ensure your greatest risks don't gamble with your retirement dreams. Ellen's risk factors include:

- Structural risk: she may be on her own putting assets aside.
- Market risk: markets and interest rates impact her.
- Tax risk: taxes are an important consideration.

We all need to consider the level of risk we're at within the three largest risks surrounding our retirement: structural, market and tax.

Your average retiree, even C-Suite level, isn't always going to understand the nuances of the tax code in comparison to their options. After all, their expertise is running their business, and a financial advisor's expertise is helping people maximize their chances of a wonderful retirement income stream.

Potential strategies for Ellen include:

- Title 26 of the US Tax Code, which pertains to how 401(k) benefits work and the tax liabilities of said code.
- Alternatives within Title 26 of the US Tax Code.
- Address structural risk: flexibility to save in ways that

benefit you.

- Address market risk: access reliable growth AND complete protection of your retirement assets.
- Address tax risk: access tax-free funds in retirement.
- Section 7702 of Title 26 of US Tax Code: Indexed Universal Life, which utilizes the power of indexing, is tax-free, and includes a death benefit.

An example of how an Indexed Universal Life (IUL) option can use dual protections in Ellen's favor:

1) Accumulate and potentially grow in IUL policy.
2) Ellen passes away earlier than expected. 3) A death benefit is paid tax-free to her heirs.

Or:

1) Accumulate and potentially grow in IUL policy.
2)Ellen retires. 3) Borrows cash value to supplement income in retirement.

As mentioned, retirement is never one-size-fits all. However, it is easy to see why Ellen's path for retirement planning could be advantageous. It saves her money, offers assurances to her children, and also allows her to retire with guarantees that may not have been possible with any other retirement option.

# How You Can Make an Informed Decision

"Be smart, be intelligent, and be informed."

*~Tony Allasandra*

THROUGH UNDERSTANDING alternative ways to invest, we are creating three legs for our retirement stool. If one leg breaks, we will no longer be left with nothing. Ensuring we have knowledgeable professionals working toward our financial betterment with this idea in mind is the best way to gain a better understanding of the market, including how we can allow the market to work for us.

Most people don't understand that tax-free strategies are how the wealthiest people in America really invest their money. The welthy don't put all their funds in danger because they want to keep it, just like the rest of us!

More and more, this is not just a strategy for those who are identified as wealthy or living in the highest tax brackets. This strategy that can work for everybody planning for retirement.

There's a demand for the information that's been shared in this book and it's no surprise it's become the focal point of the work I do with people. People need to know and understand these important details regarding retirement.

My mission is simple because I have sharing this information as the catalyst for what I do every day, so everyone can enjoy a successful retirement.

When I meet with people, I have a real, productive conversation. The objective is to help people learn information to help them to grow in their knowledge, so they can make good decisions. If they look at investments differently, they have their best chance to do better than their parents, something that seems difficult or unlikely to a great many people today.

This is a different America we live in today. Whether it's good or bad is not relevant when it comes to creating a favorable retirement scenario. Even if you're not ready to change, you should at least be ready to look at the big picture from all angles.

Advisors do two main things to help you achieve your financial goals and take you into retirement with more security.

1. Advisors, by nature, find products with great rates of return. When this happens, you are likely going to be put at a higher level of risk.
2. Advisors look for inefficiencies inside of your current portfolio that reveal where you may be losing money unknowingly and unnecessarily.

These unknown money losses are termed "unnecessary wealth transfers", and they happen most frequently within the boundaries of the following issues:

- How you pay your mortgage.
- How you fund your qualified plans.

- How you fund college for your kids, if you choose to do so or are able to do so.
- How you make your major capital purchases.

When I'm going over an important financial picture, I'm able to tap into the 'way people currently do things' and see if they are making the wisest decisions. If there is room for improvement, this information is shared with the client, so they can see ways to more favorably invest their money.

And then there are the four toughest questions that you must address, and the earlier you contemplate the questions, the more time you will have to plan properly.

1. **What rate of return do you need on your assets to be able to retire and maintain your current lifestyle?** This is where you can best determine how to approach the accumulation years for your retirement, which will be largely dependent on your starting point and the number of years you have until retirement.

2. **How much do you need to save on a monthly basis or yearly basis to retire with a comfortable lifestyle?** Depending on your job, there may be certain times of year that are easier to save. Not everyone has a consistent paycheck week after week. Through this evaluation, it's important to factor in your expected longevity, all incomes that are guaranteed, and those which may not be. Also, if possible, consider your Social Security Income (SSI) as an offset for your healthcare expenses.

3. **How long will you have to work to maintain your**

**current lifestyle?** Due to market conditions and how they impact your current investments, you may have to look at different options for when its best for you to retire. Instead of age sixty-five, you may be looking at waiting for a few more years to set up your optimal future. Certain products can help you achieve this more securely than others.

4. **By how much do you have to reduce your current lifestyle to be able to achieve a better-quality lifestyle in retirement?** It's great to want fun and nice things when you're working. They are often the rewards that make life special. However, if that $10K vacation today equates to having to work an extra two years down the road before retirement, make sure your vacation worth your time.

These questions must be asked. After all, considering what's currently happening as you live your life, compared to what you envision for your future is important. A good advisor, one with your best interests in mind, will do this at no cost to you as a service to demonstrate how they can be an asset to your retirement planning strategies.

What I love most about these consultations is how my team and I at Forecast Financial Group help alleviate the nervousness people have about their finances. They may come in feeling overwhelmed but exit with a strong picture and plan of action for the future that leaves them feeling inspired and ready.

Financial advisors should not be singular in their focus, because that isn't being of genuine service to you and your needs. Continuously educating and informing you of changes that may impact your retirement should be managed through one-on-one follow-ups, as well as valuable sources such as newsletters, client dinners, and presentations, webinars, and emails.

Imagine how empowering your financial wellbeing can be when you have a proactive advisor who reaches out to you about the latest market news and what it means to you.

Being mindful of the profound importance your financial outlook has on your life is what drives us. We do not take anything for granted when it comes to our client relationships.

As advisors, we ingest a great deal of information every day. Our job at Forecast Financial Group is to keep you as informed as possible. We remain devoted to informing and educating people on financial wellness.

As part of this commitment, we offer financial boot camps to help people learn more, faster, because the more our clients (or a consumer) knows, the more we serve our community.

Today is an important day for you. Are you going to gamble you're properly prepared for retirement? Are you willing to pay more in fees and taxes than necessary? How well do you understand what your investments are doing to help you achieve your goals?

If you're feeling uncertain or want to know that you are positioning yourself as favorably as possible, contact Forecast Financial Group. The conversation will cost you nothing, but we will offer you the chance to learn, grow, and potentially retire in a better position than you may have imagined.

# About James Hamilton

JAMES HAMILTON IS AN Army Veteran, serving America for nearly ten years prior to pursuing his entrepreneurial projects. Through the volatile markets of 2000, James learned valuable lessons about how the market could impact the most solid of plans. This inspired him, and he decided to take control of his finances and understand the best options available.

Through James' commitment to financial wellbeing, he uncovered options many financial advisors had access to but did not pursue with clients. He felt the information and strategies were too important not present to clients for consideration.

James is inspired by, and advocates for, the Biblical principles of money, which are designed to empower people by allowing their money to work optimally. According to James, "A strong family has the ability to educate, inspire, and lay out a foundation of action that can be given to future generations."

Today, as CEO of Forecast Financial Group, James leads a team committed to providing clients with financial education and resources to identify retirement goals and forge a path to create and preserve predictable income for retirement. He is also a best-selling co-author with Brian Tracy with <u>Cracking the Code to Success</u> and is expanding into financial coaching and presentations to share his philosophy. James enjoys traveling, where he works as a motivational speaker and business consultant specializing in helping the underserved black entrepreneurial community learn how to gain insight and discipline for smarter business strategies. These strategies lead to a business's prosperity and to employees increased wellbeing.

James's personal passion and professional conviction merge in his volunteer and philanthropic work. He primarily works with churches of all denominations, donating to their most cherished causes in exchange for an opportunity to connect with their parishioners to teach them the various financial strategies that will better their lives. This commitment is very dear to James's heart, as he grew up in the projects with far too few role models who understood how to rise out of their conditions.

Making his home in the Raleigh, North Carolina area, James enjoys life with his supportive and encouraging wife, Matisha and his daughter, Haniah. He is eternally grateful for both and the joy they bring into his life. In addition, he has a great many friends who have inspired and stood by him. Rod Smith is one of these friends, inspiring him with his knowledge, inspiration, and achievement of goals, including two Super Bowl rings during his time with the Denver Broncos.

As the future unfolds, James is excited to tap into all the available ways to create a better community and help people reach their fullest potentials, both in life and in retirement.

# Also by James Hamilton

————

CRACKING THE CODE TO Success, with Brian Tracy, et al.
AISN: B06ZYGJHSB

# Contact James Hamilton

———

1-800-678-2045

james@forecastfinancialgroup.com

www.ForecastFinancialGroup.com